Brain-Teasing Riddles For Curious Kids

433 Funny Riddles and Brain Teasers for Kids and Families, From Easy to Hard

Charlie Kite

Hello! Here's what's inside

Your Special Bonus

Thanks for buying this book. To show our thanks, we're giving you a special bonus book:

Family Fun Time:
67 Hilarious Riddles and Jokes

To claim your free book, go to
subscribepage.io/BonusRiddles

What Am I? Riddles

Guess the objects based on hints

1. I shrink every time you use me. What am I?

2. What has a bark but no bite?

3. The more of this there is, the less you see. What is it?

4. I have teeth, but don't bite, I help keep things tight. What am I?

5. People have stepped on me, but not many. I never stay full for long. I have a dark side. What am I?

6. I have a bow but no arrows, I have a deck but no cards, I can float but not fly. What am I?

7. I am a pet and I have four paws. I don't like cats and I say "woof". who am I?

8. I have three eyes and stand on one leg. Follow my rules or face the consequences. What am I?

9. I have a straight back and sharp teeth to cut things. What am I?

10. I give milk and have a horn, but I'm not a cow. What am I?

11. I am bought by the yard but worn by the foot. What am I?

12. I'm hard as a rock, but I melt immediately in hot water. What am I?

13. I come out at night without being called, and I'm lost in the day without being stolen. What am I?

14. You can drop me from the tallest building and I'll be ok, but if you drop me into water, I'll die. What am I?

15. People make me, save me, change me, raise me. What am I?

16. I go around and in the house, but never touch the house. What am I?

17. The person who makes it, sells it. The person who buys it, never uses it. The person who uses it, never knows they're using it. What am I?

18. I can fly without wings, cry without eyes, but wherever I go, darkness closely follows. What am I?

19. I make a loud sound when I'm changing. When I do change, I get bigger but weigh less. What am I?

20. I have no feet, no hands, no wings, but I climb to the sky. What am I?

21. What has a face and two hands, but no arms or legs?

22. What is full of holes but still holds water?

23. What has many keys but can't open a single lock?

24. What has words, but never speaks?

25. What has a bottom at the top?

26. I run in and out of town all day and night. What am I?

27. What has many teeth but can't bite?

28. What has a ring but no finger?

29. I'm light as a feather, but not even the strongest person can hold me for more than a few minutes. What am I?

30. What has a head and a tail but no body?

31. What has a thumb and four fingers but is not alive?

32. What has many needles but doesn't sew?

33. What has an eye but cannot see?

34. I'm white, and perfect for cutting and grinding. What am I?

35. I have cities, but no houses. I have mountains, but no trees. I have water, but no fish. What am I?

36. What has to be broken before you can use it?

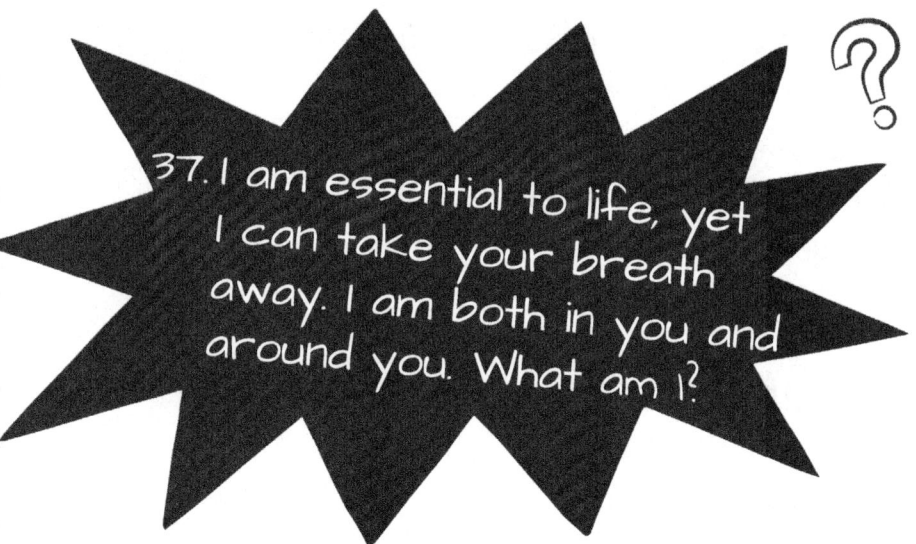

37. I am essential to life, yet I can take your breath away. I am both in you and around you. What am I?

38. What room has no door or windows?

39. I am a color, but you can eat me?

40. What kind of table can you eat?

41. I'm not alive, but I can die. What am I?

42. You are my brother, but I am not your brother. Who am I?

43. What room do ghosts avoid?

44. What building has the most stories?

45. I am made up of butter and I can fly. What am I?

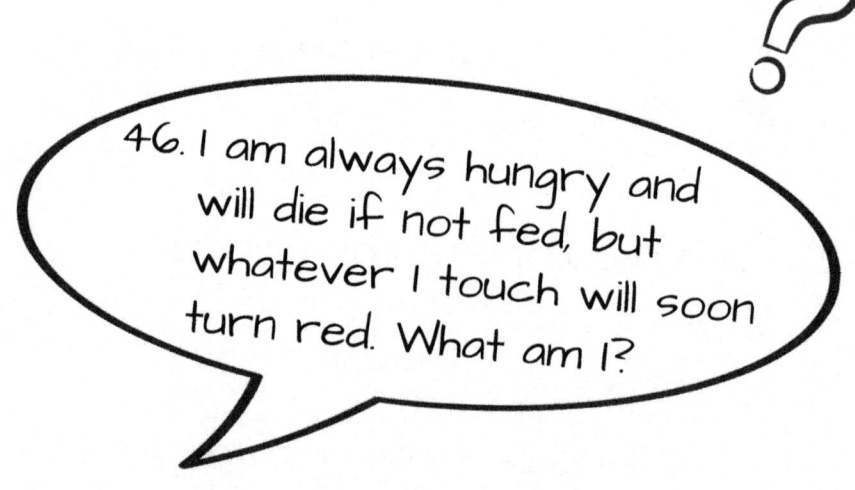

46. I am always hungry and will die if not fed, but whatever I touch will soon turn red. What am I?

47. I have branches, but no fruit, trunk or leaves. What am I?

48. I stand in one place, yet I fill a whole room. What am I?

49. I'm often running yet I have no legs. You need me to stay cool. What am I?

50. I have a tongue that can't taste, eyes that can't see, and a soul that can't feel. What am I?

51. I can be bare or covered, and I hold your weight all day. What am I?

52. I have many rings, but they are not valuable. What am I?

53. I'm not a snake, but I have a coil. I can warm you, but I'm not a blanket. What am I?

54. I roar loudly and have a big mane. I'm the king of the jungle. What am I?

55. I'm not a window but I have a pane, I'm not a door but I do have a frame. What am I?

56. I light up the night and turn off in the day, what am I?

57. I wear a jacket but have no arms, I have eyes but no face, I can be mashed or fried. What am I?

58. I'm known for my wisdom, I fly at night. I can turn my head around, not quite full circle, but almost right round. What am I?

59. I have a head, a foot, but no body. What am I?

60. I have 4 legs, but I can't walk. I have a back, but I don't lie down. What am I?

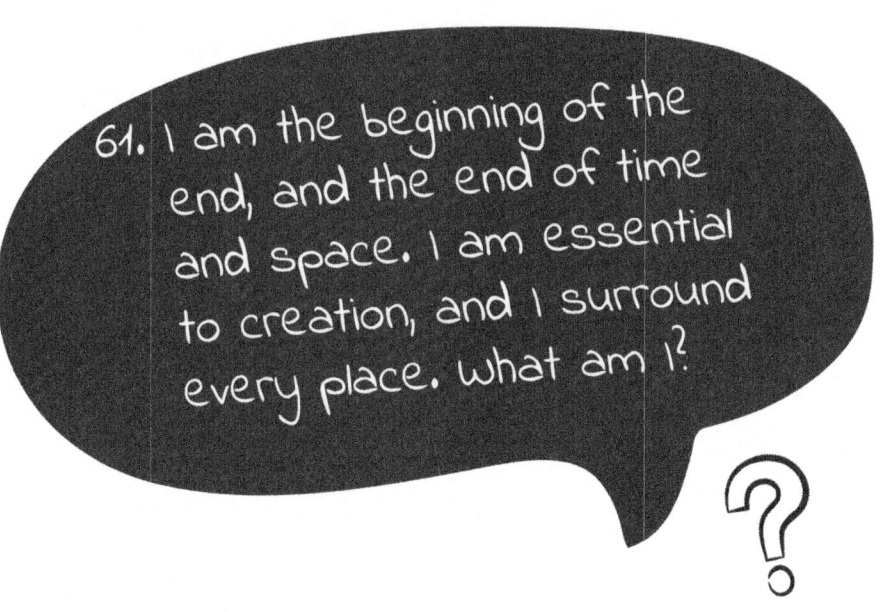

61. I am the beginning of the end, and the end of time and space. I am essential to creation, and I surround every place. What am I?

62. I am big on Saturday and Sunday. Small on Tuesday, Wednesday and Thursday. I'm not on Monday or Friday. What am I?

63. I have a long trunk and big ears. I'm the largest land animal in the world. What am I?

64. I buzz around flowers and make sweet honey. What am I?

65. I moo and give you milk. You'll find me on a farm. What am I?

66. I croak and live near ponds and lakes. I'm green and eat bugs. What am I?

67. I'm flat when I'm new. I'm fat when you use me. I release my gas when something sharp touches me. What am I?

68. I look just like you, but I'm not you. You can make me bigger or carry me in your wallet. Hang me up or give me away. What am I?

69. I am so simple that I can only point, yet I guide people all over the world. What am I?

70. I can be red or blue—I am always changing. I can ruin your day or lift you up. I am always with you except when you sleep. What am I?

71. I'm a 5-letter word. I am normally below you. If you remove my 1st letter, you'll find me above you. If you remove my 1st & 2nd letters, you can't see me. What am I?

72. What has a 1000 legs and no feet?

73. What is as big as an elephant but weighs nothing?

74. I am a colorful bird with a curved beak. I love to imitate what humans say. What am I?

75. I can fly without wings, touch the sky, yet I vanish in a blink. What am I?

76. I grow taller when I eat, but weaker when I drink. What am I?

77. What is full of holes but still holds a lot?

78. I have a stem, but I am not a flower. I have a foot, but I cannot hop. Children are too young to hold me. What am I?

79. I shave every day, but my beard stays the same. What am I?

80. You answer me, although I never ask questions. What am I?

81. No matter how little or how much you use me, you change me every month. What am I?

82. Useful for measuring or leading a country. What am I?

83. I have a ring but no finger. When you're expecting a visitor, you eagerly listen for me. What am I?

84. I sound like I could cut you, but I'm actually quite comfortable. I can be green or yellow. I can be stiff or soft. I am a friend to bugs and also bare feet. What am I?

85. I am the key to unlocking the greatest mysteries, yet I'm not a key. What am I?

86. I'm not a bird, but I can fly; I have no engine, but I can soar through the sky. What am I?

87. I can be long, like a story, or short, like a clue; I'm shared among many or just between two. What am I?

88. I have no beginning, middle or end. What am I?

89. I can be cracked, made into an omelet, or boiled. What am I?

90. I have seven rings made of rock and ice, but you cannot wear them on your fingers. They are way, way too big. What am I?

91. I'm red or green, spicy and hot, I'm in the salsa you like a lot. What am I?

92. I'm yellow inside, white outside, and protected by a green jacket. What am I?

93. I twinkle above you, in the vast sky, I'm not a plane, nor a spy. What am I?

94. Peel my layers without a tear, yet many cry when they come near. What am I?

95. I come in different colors, but I'm not a rainbow. I stick to things, but I'm not glue. You write on me, and I help you remember. What am I?

96. I can be straight or curly, long or short, I grow but I'm not a plant. What am I?

97. I make two people out of one. What am I?

98. It's good to stretch me and push my limits. The more you use me, the stronger I get. When I am sharp, I am at my best. What am I?

99. I am a ball that can be rolled but never bounced or thrown. What am I?

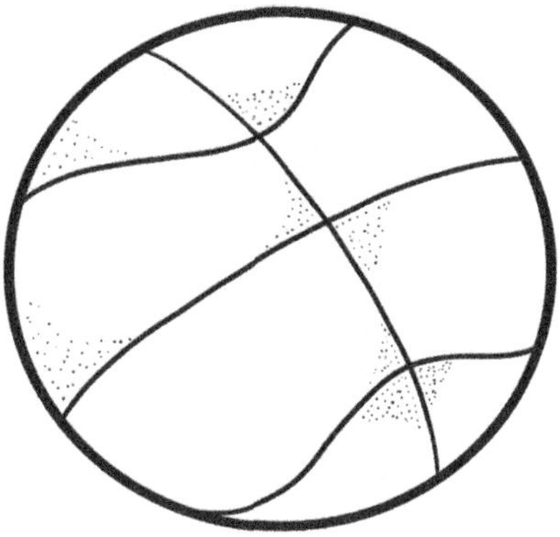

100. I get rid of mistakes. What am I?

101. If you take away one hand, some will remain. What am I?

102. I'm red and I live in your body. I'm the symbol of love. Please don't break me. What am I?

103. Please be patient. I'm new in the world. I cry a lot. Everyone smiles at me. Please pick me up. What am I?

104. I'm usually green and brown. With rain, I can live for a long time. Birds love me. What am I?

105. I wear a suit that's not for show, above the Earth, I freely go. With stars and planets I do play. Who am I that flies this way?

106. I wear dresses and sometimes a crown. In tales of old, my stories are found. I may be saved, or save the day. Who am I in this fairytale play?

107. You can touch me, but I can't touch you back. You can see me, but I only reflect you and can never reject you. What am I?

Math Riddles

Solve puzzles using numbers

1. Which number stays the same no matter what number you multiply it with?

2. 3 ducks lay 3 eggs in 3 days. How many eggs will 300 ducks lay in 300 days?

3. How many months of the year have 28 days?

4. If two's company and three's a crowd, what are four and five?

5. What number do you get when you multiply all of the numbers on a telephone's number pad?

6. There are two ducks in front of a duck, two ducks behind a duck, and a duck in the middle. How many ducks are there?

7. What three numbers, none of which are zero, give the same result whether they're added or multiplied?

8. I am thinking of a shape that has more corners than a square but fewer than an octagon. It has the same number of sides as it has corners. What shape am I thinking of?

9. Think of a number. Multiply it by 3. Add 6. Divide by 3. Subtract the number you started with. What was the number you thought of?

10. In an enchanted forest, there are 5 times as many unicorns as dragons. If the forest is home to 6 dragons, how many legs are there in the forest if each creature has 4 legs?

11. If there are 8 stars in the sky and each star is a corner of a square, how many squares are formed in the sky?

12. Elijah's piggy bank has 50 coins. If 4/5 of the coins are pennies, how many pennies does Elijah have?

13. Think of a number. Double it. Add six. Divide it by two. Subtract the number you started with. The answer is three. What was the number you thought of?

14. Jane imagines she's a time traveler. If she travels 2 hours into the future, watches a 1-hour movie, and then travels 3 hours back in time, what's the total number of hours she has traveled in her imagination?

15. If you have a jar that holds 5 cookies and you put in 2 cookies, take 1 out, then put in 3 more, and finally take out 2, how many cookies are left in the jar?

16. Sally read 2 books every week except for the last week of the month when she read only 1. How many books did she read in a month that has 4 weeks?

17. Pick a number from 1-10, multiply it by 2, add ten, divide it by 2, now subtract the number you picked from the number you've just calculated. What is it?

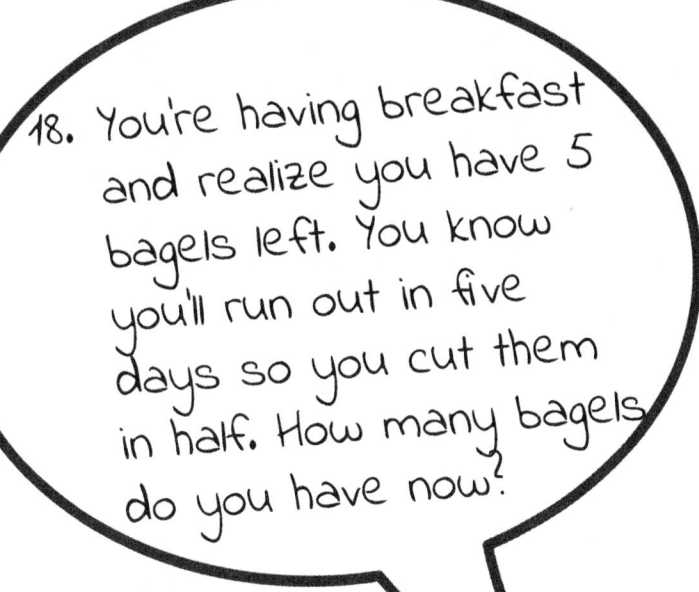

18. You're having breakfast and realize you have 5 bagels left. You know you'll run out in five days so you cut them in half. How many bagels do you have now?

19. Dave has 10 siblings, 4 boys and 6 girls. He has a mother and father. How many people are in the family?

20. James is 5 years old. Emily is also 5 years old. Theo is 4 years old. Ava is 3 years old. Charles is 7 years old. Benjamin is 8. How old is Michael?

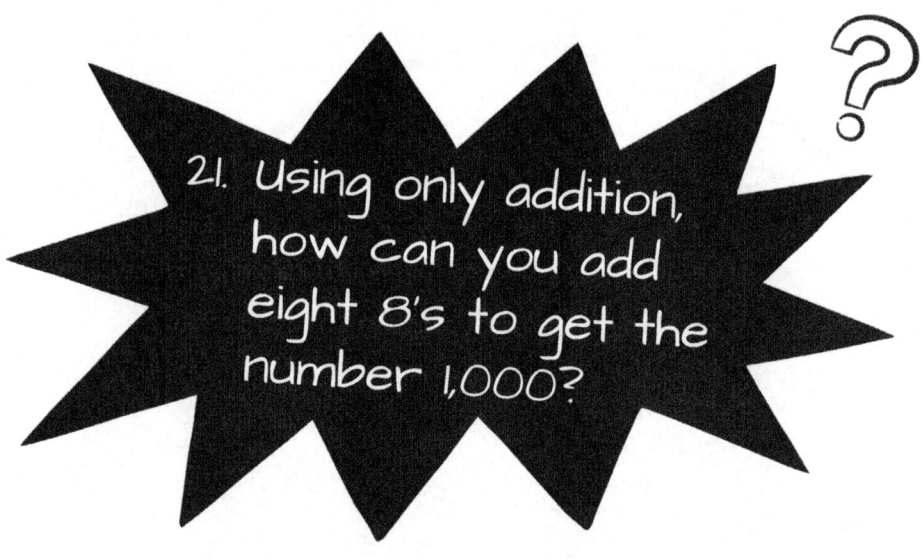

21. Using only addition, how can you add eight 8's to get the number 1,000?

22. When Peter was 8, his brother was half his age. Now, Peter is 14. How old is his brother?

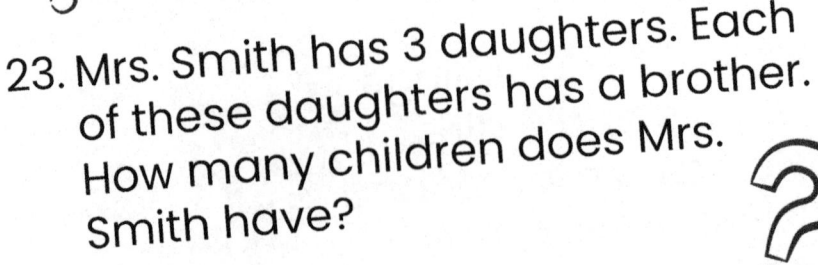

23. Mrs. Smith has 3 daughters. Each of these daughters has a brother. How many children does Mrs. Smith have?

24. A new clothing store has a special way of pricing items. A vest costs $20, a tie costs $15, a blouse costs $30, and underwear costs $45. How much would pants cost?

25. A chicken and egg together cost $1.06. The chicken costs $1 more than the egg. How much does the egg cost?

26. The ages of a father and son add up to 66. The father's age is the son's age reversed. How old could they be?

27. What two whole, positive numbers have a one-digit answer when multiplied and a two-digit answer when added?

28. If 1=5, 2=15, 3=215, and 4=3215. What does 5 equal?

29. What two whole, positive numbers have the same answer when multiplied together as when added together?

30. If three cats catch three mice in three minutes, how many cats would be needed to catch 100 mice in 100 minutes?

31. If 5 hens lay 5 eggs in 5 days, how many eggs will 15 hens lay in 15 days?

32. Think of a number. Double it. Add ten. Half it. Subtract the original number. What do you get?

33. A farmer has 15 cows and all but 8 wander off into the woods. How many cows are left on the farm?

34. I have 5 apples in one hand and 6 apples in the other. What do I have?

35. There are 7 ducks in a pond. 2 decide to swim away. How many are left in the pond?

36. There are 10 fish in a tank, 2 swim away, 4 die, and 3 come back to life. How many fish are there?

37. There are 4 wheels on a car. If there are 5 cars in the parking lot, how many wheels are there in total?

38. Your sock drawer contains 19 white socks and 19 blue socks. If you can't look while choosing, what is the smallest number of socks you must pull out to ensure you have at least one matching pair?

39. There are 10 pencils in a box. If you take 4 out and then put 2 back, how many pencils are in the box?

40. If you divide 100 by half, what's the answer?

41. Lily has 3 pink flowers, 4 red flowers, and 2 yellow flowers. How many flowers does she have in total?

42. There are 12 eggs in a dozen. If you have 2 dozen, how many eggs do you have?

43. If you find 3 seashells on the beach every day for 4 days, how many seashells do you have?

44. If you toss a coin 50 times and it lands heads up every time, what is the chance it will land heads up on your next throw?

45. There are 12 cookies in a jar. If you ate 1/4 of the cookies, how many cookies would be left in the jar?

46. Four times this number is a century and twice is half a century. What number is it?

47. A farmer had 28 pigs. He sold 1/4 of them at the market. How many pigs did the farmer have left?

48. Mom baked 32 cookies. Dad ate 1/8 of the cookies. How many cookies did Dad eat?

49. There are 30 students in a class. 2/5 of the students are boys. How many boys are in the class?

50. Lucas had $16 to spend at the fair. He spent 1/2 of his money on rides and 1/4 of his money on food. How much money did he have left?

51. The basketball team played 24 games this season. They won 3/4 of their games. How many games did they win?

52. I am endless and boundless. I look like a sleeping 8 number. What am I?

53. There are 45 students going on a field trip. Each bus can hold 15 students. How many buses will they need?

54. Harper had 36 stickers. She gave 1/3 of her stickers to her friend Ava. How many stickers did Harper have left?

55. You plant sunflower seeds in your garden, and each day the number of flowers doubles. If the garden is full of flowers on the 52nd day, on which day was it half full?

56. How many seconds are there in one year?

57. There are 10 apples in a basket. Ten people each take 1 apple, but there is still 1 apple in the basket. How can this be?

58. I add 5 to 9 and get 2. The answer is correct, so what am I?

59. Billy is 100 cm tall, and his friend Theo is 1000mm tall. Who is taller?

60. How many times can you subtract 10 from 25?

61. I am bigger than 50 and equal to the total number of weeks in a year. What number am I?

Word Play Riddles

Play with words to find answers

1. A boy tells his friend, “I challenge you to a test. I can write your exact weight on this piece of paper”. His friend accepts the challenge. There were no scales to weigh his friend. How did the boy win the challenge?

2. What breaks yet never falls, and what falls yet never breaks?

3. What kind of dog never bites?

4. How can a leopard move its spots?

5. How far will a fox run into the woods?

6. Can you name three consecutive days without using Wednesday, Friday, and Sunday?

7. How can you take 2 from 5 and leave 4?

8. How do you spell dog backwards?

9. What is seen in the middle of March and April?

10. What do Alexander the Great and Winnie the Pooh have in common?

11. What is always coming but never arrives?

12. What starts with a W and ends with a T

13. What 11-letter English word is always pronounced incorrectly?

14. What type of dress can never be worn?

15. Why can't a nose be 12 inches long?

16. It belongs to you, but your friends use it more.

17. There's only one word in the dictionary that's spelled wrong.

18. Forwards I'm heavy. Backwards I'm not.

19. What gets sharper the more you use it?

20. What five-letter word has one left when two letters are removed?

21. You see me once in June, twice in November, but not at all in May.

22. I am an odd number. Take away one letter, and I become even.

23. What 5-letter word becomes shorter when you add two letters to it?

24. Take away the whole and some still remains.

25. How do you spell COW in thirteen letters?

26. What has no body and no nose?

27. What question can someone ask all day long, always get completely different answers, and yet all the answers could be correct?

28. What two things can you never eat for breakfast?

29. Which one of Santa's reindeer can you see in outer space?

30. What do you call a bear with no teeth?

31. What has 4 eyes but can't see?

32. You draw a line. Without touching it, how do you make the line longer?

33. Which eight-letter word still remains a word after removing each letter from it?

34. Can you name the two days starting with T besides Tuesday and Thursday?

35. A monkey, a squirrel, and a bird are racing to the top of a coconut tree. Who will get the banana first - the monkey, the squirrel, or the bird?

36. A man walks into a bar and immediately falls unconscious. Why?

37. What is the center of Gravity?

38. What is faster hot or cold?

39. What do you call a person who is afraid of Santa Claus?

40. What Jack has a head but no body?

41. When was the latest year that is the same upside down?

42. What kind of key do you use on Thanksgiving?

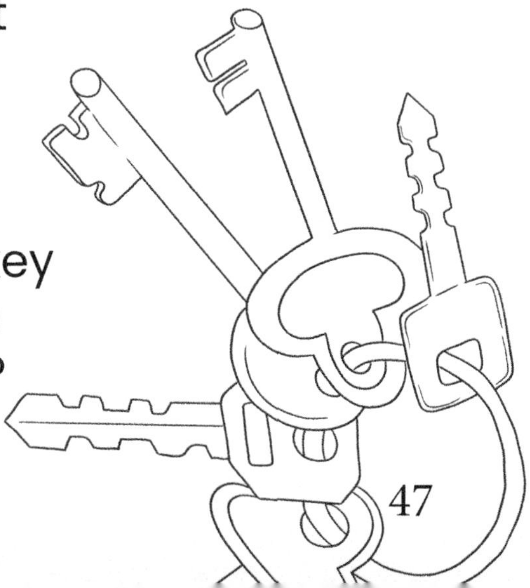

43. What can fill a room but takes up no space?

44. What do you call a fruit that is never alone?

45. What color is the wind?

46. What fruit has its seeds on the outside?

47. What do you get when you cross a black cat and a lemon?

48. What kind of ears does an engine have?

49. Why didn't the skeleton cross the road?

50. What do you call a fish with no eyes?

51. How can you say rabbit without using the letter R?

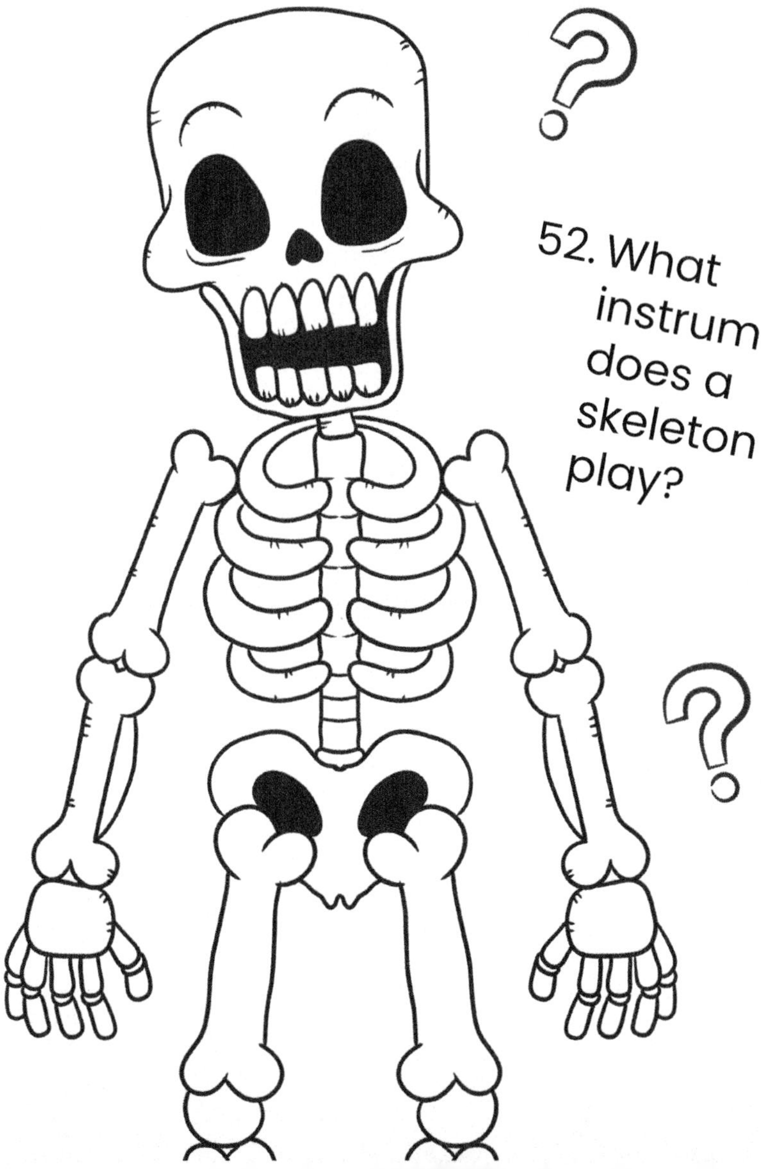

52. What instrument does a skeleton play?

53. Are you smart? "Yes". How do you spell it? "_____"

54. What does it take to make an octopus laugh?

55. What word does not belong in this list: hold, told, scold, gold, or mold?

56. What kind of cheese is made backwards?

57. What kind of cup doesn't hold water?

58. What's bright orange with green on top and sounds like a parrot?

59. What's the capital of France?

60. What can you put between 6 and 7, to make the result greater than 6, but less than 7?

61. What do the numbers 11, 69, and 88 all have in common?

62. I come once in a year, twice in a week, but never in a day.

63. I am a word that begins with the letter "I." If you add the letter "A" to me, I become a new word with a different meaning, but that sounds exactly the same.

64. What letter of
the alphabet
appears at
the start of
questions?

65. What question can you never answer "yes" to?

66. What would you find in the middle of Toronto?

67. What word is pronounced the same if you take away four of its five letters?

68. What is at the end of everything?

69. What English word has three consecutive double letters?

70. How do you make the word "one" disappear?

71. Which fish costs the most?

72. What word doesn't belong in this group? That, hat, what, mat, cat, sat, pat, chat?

73. Y-E-S spells YES, what does E-Y-E-S spell?

74. Which does not belong in this group: Apple, Grape, Banana, Cherry, Pear?

75. You are in a cold room and you want to get warm. How do you get warm?

76. What familiar word starts with IS, ends with AND, and has LA in the middle?

77. How do you spot a modern spider?

78. What kind of lion never roars?

79. What kind of shoes are made of banana skins?

80. What 10-letter word starts with gas?

81. What kind of running means walking?

82. What part of London is in France?

83. Why is Europe like a frying pan?

84. What kind of bees make milk?

85. If two snakes marry, what will their towels say?

86. What table has not a leg to stand on?

87. What can you hold without touching it?

Logic Riddles

Solve the riddles with your logic skills

1. How much dirt is in a hole that measures six feet by six feet by five feet?

2. Three different doctors said that Jack is their brother yet Jack says he has no brothers. Who is lying?

3. A plane crashed between the border of Germany and France. Where were the survivors buried?
??

4. If an electric train is traveling south, which way is the smoke going?

5. Two fathers and two sons went for pizza. Each person had a slice, but only 3 slices were eaten. How?

6. You see a boat filled with people. It has not sunk, but when you look again, you don't see a single person on the boat. Why?

7. Cats have four, Dogs have four, but school has six. What are they?

8. There's a one-story house where everything is red. The walls are red. The doors are red. Even all the furniture is red. The house has red beds and red couches. What color are the stairs?

9. If you're running in a race and you pass the person in second place, what place are you in now?

10. Before Mount Everest was discovered, what was the highest mountain on Earth?

11. Two boys have the same parents and were born at the same hour on the same day of the same month, but they are not twins. How?

12. A woman has 7 kids. Half of them are boys. How is this possible?

13. Emma's mother has three children, Snap, Crackle, and _________ ?

14. If you don't keep me, I'll break. What am I?

15. What can you hear, but not see or touch, even though you control it?

16. What always goes up but never goes down?

17. How can you get 8 horses in seven stables?

18. How can a 10 year old girl go 50 days without sleep?

19. What loses its head every morning but gets it back every night?

20. If you have three apples and you take away two, how many do you have?

21. How can you leave a room with two legs and return with six legs?

22. If a rooster laid a brown egg and a white egg, what kind of chicks would hatch?

23. What is moving left to right, right now?

24. How did the soccer fan know before the game that the score would be 0-0?

25. Which one of Santa's reindeer is the fastest?

26. Ridley was born in February, Brody was born in January, and Charlie in May. Who is the oldest?

27. If fish lived on land, where would they live?

28. What four-legged animal can jump higher than a house?

29. What two keys are the hardest to turn?

30. What is next in this sequence: JFMAMJJASON_ ?

31. One night, a butcher, a baker, and a candlestick maker go to a hotel. When they get their bill, it's for four people. Who's the fourth person?

32. An employee works at the butcher shop, he is five feet eleven inches tall, and he wears size 10 sneakers. What does he weigh?

33. How many of each type of animal did Moses take on the Ark?

34. A panda is heavier than a raccoon. A lion is heavier than a panda. A tiger is heavier than a lion. Which is lighter, a tiger or a panda?

35. Two girls were born to the same mother, on the same day, at the same time, in the same month and year and yet they're not twins. How is that possible?

36. Mr. Blue lives in a blue house, Mrs. Green lives in a green house, and Mr. Red lives in a red house. Who lives in the White House?

37. When I point up it's bright, but when I point down it's dark. What am I?

38. You're in a room and there is a ghost in the room, but you're the only one in the room. How is this possible?

39. Justin is turning 10 this year, yet he turned 9 yesterday. How is this possible?

40. When is homework not homework?

41. Your mom has 4 kids, one named North, another named South, and one East. What is the last child's name?

42. Which side of the turkey has the most feathers?

43. A man was pushing his car along the road when he came to a hotel. He shouts "I'm bankrupt!" Why did the man shout that out?

44. What do dogs have that no other animal has?

45. What has four wheels and flies?

46. I am the beginning of everything, the end of everywhere. I'm the beginning of eternity, the end of time and space. What am I?

47. What is 3/7 chicken, 2/3 cat and 2/4 goat?

48. Charlotte threw a ball as hard as she could and it came back to her, without anything or anyone touching it. How?

49. A cowboy rode into town on Friday. He stayed for three nights and rode out on Friday. How is this possible?

50. A student asked his teacher, "Miss, is it fair if I get in trouble for something I did not do?" The teacher replied, "Of course not! Tell me who got you in trouble for something you didn't do?" What do you think the student replied with?

51. Two twins live together all the time. They see the whole world, but never see each other. Can you explain?

52. A woman was born in 1868 She is still alive now at the age of 26 How is this possible?

53. What do both a tooth and a tree have?

54. What has a thousand needles but can't sew?

55. If it takes 2 people to dig 1 hole how many people does it take to dig 1/2 a hole?

56. What has 4 letters and sometimes 9, never has 5 letters and always has 6 letters. What is the answer?

57. If a farmer has 3 horses, 2 ducks, 1 pig and a wife, how many feet are on his farm?

58. George, Helen, and Steve are drinking coffee. Ben, Beth and Dave are drinking water. Using logic, is Elizabeth drinking coffee or water?

59. Is it possible to make up a sentence that ends with the letter I?

60. If you threw a white stone into the red sea, what would it become?

61. There are 30 cows in a field, and 28 chickens. How many didn't?

62. What has 13 hearts, but no other organs?

63. Where does one wall meet the other wall?

64. A penguin in Antarctica is called Andrew. A penguin in New Zealand is called Neville. What do you call a penguin in Dubai?

65. Mia goes to the supermarket to buy 10 tomatoes. Unfortunately, on the way back home, all but 9 get ruined. How many tomatoes are left in good condition?

66. There is a bus full of people traveling to New York and no one gets off the bus throughout the journey. But when it gets to New York there is not a single person left. How is this possible?

67. A bus driver goes the wrong way down a one-way street. He passes the cops, but they don't stop him. Why?

Joke Riddles

Laugh at funny questions and answers

1. What time does a tennis player get up?

2. What is cut on a table but is never eaten?

3. What do race car drivers eat for breakfast?

4. What did one math book say to the other math book?

5. What do you throw out when you want to use it but take in when you don't want to use it?

6. What comes down but never goes up?

7. What do ghosts use to wash their hair?

8. In what school do you learn to greet people?

9. What has one eye but can't see?

10. What can travel all around the world without leaving its corner?

11. Where does today come before yesterday?

12. What is red and smells like blue paint?

13. What goes up and down but doesn't move?

14. What is so fragile that saying its name breaks it?

15. What did the zero say to the eight?

16. What comes once in a minute, twice in a moment, but never in a thousand years?

17. What fruit can you never cheer up?

18. What starts with "P", ends with "E", and has thousands of letters?

19. What gets bigger when more is taken away?

20. What kind of band never plays music?

21. What kind of key opens a banana?

22. What is at the end of every rainbow?

23. What can be cracked, made, told and played?

24. What are the biggest kind of ants?

25. The more you take, the more you leave behind. What am I?

26. What has a heart that doesn't beat?

27. What can you hold in your left hand but not in your right?

28. When spelled forwards, I'm part of your daily life; spelled backwards, I'm something you dislike. What am I?

29. What do you get if you cross a vampire and a snowman?

30. Where do cows go for their holidays?

31. Your reflection can be seen here, as long as you're not moving?

32. What invention lets you look right through a wall?

33. What letter of the alphabet has the most water?

34. What did the baseball glove say to the ball?

35. Why did Tigger go to the bathroom?

36. Why was the broom late?

37. What's the best way to catch a fish?

38. What weighs more, a pound of feathers or a pound of stones?

39. What is the richest nut?

40. Why can't a pirate ever finish the alphabet?

41. Why does the teacher wear sunglasses when she's in the classroom?

42. What did the bee say to the flower?

43. Where do fish keep their money?

44. What is the last thing you take off before bed?

45. Why don't eggs tell jokes?

46. Why do bees hum?

47. What did the triangle say to the circle?

48. How do you fit 5 elephants in a compact car?

49. Where does a 500-pound gorilla sleep?

50. How do bees get to school?

51. What food lives at the beach?

52. Why did the tortilla chip start dancing?

53. Why was the math book sad?

54. What happened to the broken-down frog?

55. Why do skeletons go on vacations alone?

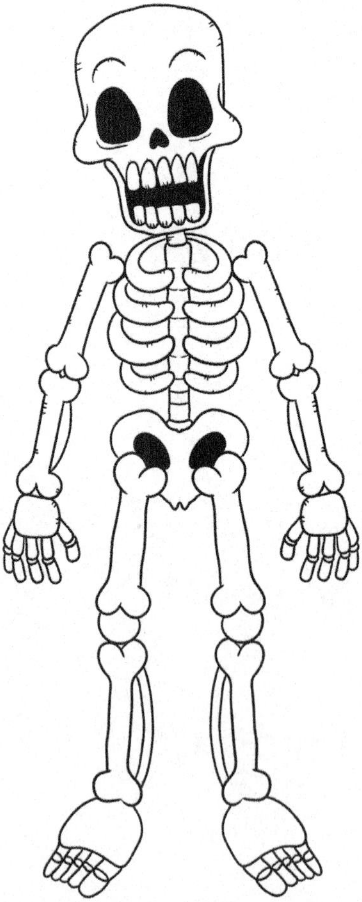

56. Where do you take a sick pirate ship?

57. Where can you learn to make ice cream?

58. Why couldn't Goldilocks sleep?

59. How do you make a poisonous snake cry?

60. How do vampires like their food served?

61. How do spiders communicate?

62. What kind of cake does a mouse eat on its birthday?

63. Where do books sleep?

64. What is the best present you can receive for Christmas?

65. Where do baby ghosts go while their parents work?

66. What is a ghost's favorite dessert?

67. What animal is the best at baseball?

68. Who was the most famous skeleton detective?

69. What kind of lion never roars?

70. Why are teddy bears never hungry?

71. What happened to Einstein when he took a shower?

72. Why does a person who is sick lose his sense of touch?

73. What is black and white and has 16 wheels?

74. What kind of bars won't keep a prisoner in jail?

75. Why did the student eat his homework?

76. Why did the belt go to jail?

77. Why did the cookie go to the doctors?

78. What does S-H-O-P spell? What does P-R-O-P spell? What does C-R-O-P spell? What does D-R-O-P spell? What do you do at a green light?

79. What tastes better than it smells?

80. What is in front of a woman and at the end of a cow?

81. Why did the football team go to the bank?

82. What is a tree's favorite drink?

83. Why is the Moon like a dollar?

84. What did the pencil say to the other pencil?

85. Why is the baseball field hot after a game?

86. Why aren't elephants allowed on the beach?

87. Why was 6 afraid of 7?

88. What kind of coat is best put on wet?

89. What's black and white and red all over?

90. What kind of tree can you carry in your hand?

91. How can you make pants last?

92. What is it called when a dinosaur scores a goal?

93. Who wears shoes while sleeping?

94. why is the letter D like a sailor?

95. Why did the golfer put on a second pair of pants?

96. What happens when a sheep studies karate?

97. What did the sea say to the sand?

98. What is the fastest way to double your money?

99. Why couldn't the pirate play cards?

100. One word in this sentence is misspelled. What word is it?

101. What do you get if you cross a hen with a guitar?

102. Why did the spider get a job in marketing?

103. What shoes do frogs wear in the summer?

104. What do you serve that you can't eat?

105. What is a cheerleader's favorite cereal?

106. If two kids share eight pieces of chocolate cake, and one kid only gets to eat one piece, what does the other get?

107. What kind of garden does a baker have?

108. Where do cows go for fun?

109. When is a pig like ink?

110. What do you call a magician who lost his magic?

111. Who is the boss in the dairy factory?

112. What subject in school is easy for a witch?

113. Why did the chicken cross the playground?

114. What's the worst season of the year for tightrope walkers?

115. What driver never gets arrested?

116. Why did Snap, Crackle, and Pop get scared?

117. What gets wetter the more it dries?

118. How do you make anti-freeze?

Answers

What Am I? Riddles

1. Soap
2. A tree
3. Darkness
4. A zipper
5. The moon
6. A ship
7. A dog
8. A traffic light
9. A saw
10. A milk truck
11. Carpet
12. An ice cube
13. Stars
14. Paper
15. Money
16. The sun
17. A coffin
18. A cloud
19. Popcorn
20. Smoke
21. A clock
22. A sponge
23. A piano
24. A book
25. A leg
26. A road
27. A comb
28. A telephone
29. Breath
30. A coin
31. A glove
32. A Christmas tree or pine tree
33. A hurricane

34. A tooth
35. A map
36. An egg
37. Water
38. A mush-room
39. An orange
40. A veg-table
41. A battery
42. Your sister
43. The living room
44. A library
45. Butterfly
46. Fire
47. A bank
48. A lamp
49. A fan
50. A shoe
51. A foot
52. A tree
53. A heater
54. A lion
55. A picture
56. The moon
57. A potato
58. An owl
59. A bed
60. A chair
61. The letter E. End, timeE, spacE, Every placE
62. The letter S
63. An elephant
64. A bee
65. A cow
66. A frog
67. A balloon
68. Your photo
69. A compass
70. Your mood

71. Chair. Hair. Air
72. 500 pairs of pants
73. An elephant's shadow
74. A parrot
75. A bubble
76. Fire
77. A net
78. A wine glass
79. A barber
80. A telephone
81. A calendar
82. A ruler
83. A doorbell
84. A blade of grass
85. Knowledge
86. A kite
87. A conversation
88. A circle or ring
89. An egg
90. Saturn
91. A chili pepper
92. Corn
93. A star
94. An onion
95. A sticky note
96. Hair
97. A mirror
98. Your brain
99. An eyeball
100. An eraser
101. Handsome
102. Heart
103. A baby
104. A tree
105. Astronaut
106. Princess
107. A mirror

Answers

Math Riddles

1. Zero
2. 30,000 eggs
3. All of them. Every month has at least 28 days
4. Nine (4+5)
5. Zero because any number multiplied by zero is zero
6. Three ducks
7. One, two, and three (1+2+3 = 6 and 1x2x3 = 6)
8. A hexagon
9. The answer is always 2.
10. 144 legs
11. 2 squares
12. 40 pennies
13. The answer is always 3.
14. Six hours (2 forward, 1 for the movie, 3 backward)
15. Two cookies.
16. 7 books (2 books each for the first 3 weeks and 1 book in the last week)
17. Do you have 5?
18. 5 bagels
19. 13 people are in the family. Dave and his 10 siblings, his mom and dad.

20. Michael is 7 because each person's age is the same number of letters in their name
21. 888 + 88 + 8 + 8 + 8 = 1,000
22. His brother is 10
23. Mrs. Smith has 4 children
24. $25. The pricing method charges $5 for each letter needed to spell the item
25. The egg costs $0.03 and the chicken costs $1.03
26. 3 possible solutions. 51 and 15. 42 and 24. 60 and 06.
27. 1 and 9
28. 5=1
29. 2 and 2
30. The same three cats would do. Since these three cats are averaging one mouse per minute, given 100 minutes, the cats could catch 100 mice.
31. 15 eggs
32. Five
33. 8 cows
34. Big hands
35. 7 (deciding doesn't mean they left)

36. 10 (fish can't swim away in a tank and the dead ones are still in the tank)
37. 20 wheels
38. 3
39. 8 pencils
40. 200. 100 divided by 1/2
41. 9 flowers
42. 24 eggs
43. 12 seashells
44. 50/50. Previous tosses do not affect the outcome; the probability of getting heads or tails remains equal each time.
45. 9 cookies
46. 25
47. 21 pigs
48. 4 cookies
49. 12 boys
50. $4 left
51. 18 games
52. Infinity ∞
53. 3 buses
54. 24 stickers
55. 51st day
56. 12. Every month has a 2nd.
57. The 10th person took the basket with 1 apple still in it
58. A clock. When it is 9 a.m., adding 5 hours would make it 2 p.m.

59. They are both the same height. 1cm equals 10mm.

60. Once. After you subtract 10 from 25 the first time, it becomes 15.

61. 52

Answers

Wordplay Riddles

1. The boy wrote "your exact weight" on the paper
2. Day breaks, night falls
3. A hot dog
4. By moving from one place to another
5. Only halfway, because if it runs any further, it would be running out of the woods
6. Yesterday, today, and tomorrow
7. F I V E. Remove the letters F and E to leave IV, the Roman numeral for four
8. D-o-g- b-a-c-k-w-a-r-d-s
9. The letter R
10. Their middle names
11. Tomorrow
12. That's correct, it does
13. Incorrectly
14. An address
15. Because it would be a foot
16. Your name
17. The word wrong

18. Ton
19. Your brain
20. Stone
21. The letter E
22. Seven
23. Short(er)
24. The word "wholesome"
25. SEE O DOUBLE YOU
26. Nobody knows
27. What time is it?
28. Lunch and dinner
29. Comet
30. Gummy bear
31. Mississippi
32. Draw a shorter line next to it
33. Starting-Staring-String-Sting-Sing-Sin-In-I
34. Today and tomorrow
35. None of them. You can't get a banana from a coconut tree
36. It was a metal bar
37. The letter V
38. Hot, because you can easily catch a cold
39. Claus-trophobic
40. Jack-o-lantern
41. 1961
42. A Turkey
43. Light
44. A pear
45. Blew
46. A strawberry

47. A Sour Puss
48. Engineers
49. Because it didn't have the guts
50. Fsh
51. Bunny
52. A Trombone
53. I-t
54. Ten-tickles
55. Or
56. Edam
57. Cupcake or hiccup
58. A carrot
59. The letter F
60. A decimal point
61. They all read the same way when placed upside down
62. The letter E
63. Isle, add "A" to make "aisle"
64. The letter Y
65. Are you asleep yet?
66. The letter O
67. Queue
68. The letter G
69. Bookkeeper
70. Add a "G" in front and it's gone
71. A goldfish
72. What, it's pronounced differently
73. Not E-YES, Eyes
74. The Banana, it's the only one that needs peeling before eating

75. Go into the corner. It's always 90 degrees
76. Island
77. It has a website
78. A dandelion
79. Slippers
80. Automobile
81. Running out of gas!
82. The letter N
83. Because it has Greece at the bottom
84. Boobies!
85. Hiss and Hers
86. Multiplication table
87. A conversation

Answers

Logic Riddles

1. None, holes are empty
2. No one is lying because the three doctors are Jack's sisters
3. They weren't. Survivors don't need to be buried
4. There's no smoke because it's an electric train
5. There's a grandfather, a father, and his son
6. All the people were below deck
7. Letters
8. There aren't any stairs—it's a one-story house.
9. Second place
10. Mount Everest. It just hadn't been discovered yet
11. They were born in different years
12. ALL the children are boys, so half are boys and so is the other half
13. Emma
14. A promise

15. Your voice
16. Your age
17. Put the number and letter in each stable. 8/h/o/r/s/e/s
18. She sleeps at night
19. A pillow
20. You have the two you took away
21. Bring a chair back with you
22. Roosters don't lay eggs
23. Your eyes
24. The score is always 0-0 before the game
25. Dasher
26. You can't tell. We do not know the year when they were born
27. In Finland
28. Any, houses can't jump
29. Donkey and monkey
30. The letter D
31. The (k)night
32. Meat
33. None, because it was Noah, not Moses, who took animals onto the Ark
34. A panda
35. They are triplets
36. The President
37. A light switch

38. You're the ghost
39. Justin's birthday is on December 31st, the last day of the year. The current day was January 1st of the next year
40. When it's done at school
41. Your name, it's your mom, you're one of the 4 kids
42. The outside
43. He was playing monopoly
44. Puppies
45. A garbage truck
46. The letter E
47. Chicago
48. She threw the ball straight up into the air
49. His horse's name is Friday
50. Miss, I forgot to do my Homework again!
51. They're eyes
52. She was born in room 1868 in the hospital
53. Roots
54. A porcupine
55. You can't dig 1/2 a hole because once you begin to dig it is a hole
56. The word "what" has 4 letters, the word "sometimes"

has 9 letters, the word "never" has 5 letters, and the word "always" has 6 letters

57. 24 feet on his farm
58. Elizabeth is drinking coffee. The letter E appears twice in her name, as it does in the names of the others that are drinking coffee
59. The question is the answer: Is it possible to make up a sentence that ends with the letter I
60. Wet
61. 10. 20 ATE chickens so 10 cows didn't eat any chickens
62. A deck of cards
63. On the corner
64. Lost
65. Nine
66. They are all married
67. He was walking

Answers

Joke Riddles

1. Ten-ish
2. A deck of cards
3. Fast food
4. We need to divide and conquer!
5. An anchor
6. Rain
7. Sham-boo
8. Hi-school
9. A needle
10. A stamp
11. In a dictionary
12. Red paint
13. A staircase
14. Silence
15. Nice belt!
16. The letter M
17. A blueberry
18. Post Office
19. A hole
20. A rubber band
21. A monkey
22. The letter W
23. A joke
24. Gi-ants
25. Footsteps
26. An artichoke
27. Your right elbow
28. Live / Evil
29. Frostbite
30. Moo York
31. Water

32. A window
33. The letter C
34. Catch you later
35. He wanted to find his friend, Pooh!
36. It overswept
37. Have someone throw it to you
38. They both weigh a pound
39. A cash-ew
40. Because he always gets lost at sea
41. Because the students are bright
42. Hi, honey!
43. In a river bank
44. Your feet off the floor
45. Because they might crack up
46. They don't know the words
47. You're pointless
48. Two in the front, two in the back and one in the trunk
49. Wherever it wants
50. By school buzz
51. A sand-wich
52. Because they put on the salsa
53. Because it had too many problems
54. It got toad away

55. Because they have no-body to go with
56. To the doc(k)
57. In sundae school
58. Because of nightbears
59. Take away its rattle
60. In bite-size pieces
61. Through the worldwide web
62. Cheesecake
63. Under their covers
64. A broken drum, you can't beat it
65. To day scare
66. I-scream
67. A bat
68. Sherlock Bones
69. A sea lion
70. Because they are stuffed
71. He was brain-washed
72. Because he does not feel well
73. A zebra on roller skates
74. Chocolate bars
75. Because it was a piece of cake
76. For holding up a pair of pants
77. It felt crummy
78. Go
79. A tongue
80. The letter W

81. To get a quarter back
82. Root beer
83. Because it has 4 quarters
84. You're looking sharp
85. All the fans left
86. They can't keep their trunks up
87. Because 7, 8 (ate), 9
88. A coat of paint
89. A newspaper
90. A palm tree
91. Make the coats and shirts first
92. A dino-score
93. A horse
94. It follows the C (sea)
95. He got a hole in one
96. A lamb chop
97. Nothing, he just waved
98. Place it in front of the mirror
99. Because he was standing on the deck
100. Misspelled
101. A chicken that plucks itself
102. Because it was a great web designer
103. Open toad shoes
104. A tennis ball
105. Cheer-ios
106. A stomach ache

107. A flour garden
108. The moo-vies
109. When you put it in a pen
110. Ian
111. The big cheese
112. Spelling
113. To get to the other slide
114. The Fall
115. A screwdriver
116. They heard there was a cereal killer on the loose
117. A towel
118. Take away her blanket

Me and my 3 boys

A Special Request

Thanks so much for reading my book! As a small independent publisher, your support means the world to me. I hope you found it fun and entertaining, and that it gave your brain a little workout.

If you have a minute, I'd love to hear your honest feedback on Amazon. Your reviews really help and I enjoy hearing about your experience with the book.

To leave your feedback:

1. Open your camera app
2. Point your phone at the QR code below
3. The review page will pop up in your browser

Printed in Great Britain
by Amazon

51974867R00066